Exploring
Infrastructure

WASTE
MANAGEMENT

Kevin Reilly

Enslow Publishing
101 W. 23rd Street
Suite 240
New York, NY 10011
USA

enslow.com

Published in 2020 by Enslow Publishing, LLC.
101 W. 23rd Street, Suite 240, New York, NY 10011

Library of Congress Cataloging-in-Publication Data

Names: Reilly, Kevin, author.
Title: Waste management / Kevin Reilly.
Description: New York : Enslow Publishing, 2020. | Series: Exploring infrastructure | Audience: Grade 3-6. | Includes bibliographical references and index.
Identifiers: LCCN 2018022671 | ISBN 9781978503397 (library bound) | ISBN 9781978505148 (pbk.)
Subjects: LCSH: Refuse and refuse disposal—Juvenile literature.
Classification: LCC TD792 .R44 2019 | DDC 628.4—dc23
LC record available at https://lccn.loc.gov/2018022671

Printed in the United States of America

To Our Readers: We have done our best to make sure all website addresses in this book were active and appropriate when we went to press. However, the author and the publisher have no control over and assume no liability for the material available on those websites or on any websites they may link to. Any comments or suggestions can be sent by email to customerservice@enslow.com.

CONTENTS

INTRODUCTION

A World Without Waste Management

People today create a huge amount of waste. Waste is any unwanted or unusable material that needs to be discarded. Think about the trash that your family throws away every week. Now think of the millions of people who live in the United States alone. All of those people create waste as well. What do we do with all of that waste? We have invented a system that oversees the collection, transportation, treatment, and disposal of it. It is called waste management. Waste management is one of the most important systems in any town or city. It keeps the streets, air, and water clean.

In order to see how important waste management is, let's imagine what life would be like without it. Starting tomorrow, garbage will no longer be collected from your curb. If you live in America, it probably won't take long before this becomes a huge problem for your family. America creates more waste than any other country in the world: 4.4 pounds (2 kilograms) per person, every single day.

Trash piles up during a garbage strike in Paris.

That's more than 1,600 pounds (725 kg) of waste per person each year. As a whole, the United States makes more than 250 million tons (226.8 metric tons) of waste every year. That would be the same weight as 1.2 million blue whales! If we lined all of that garbage up, it could stretch to the moon and back twenty-five times!

Just over half of the waste made in the United is municipal solid waste. This means household garbage and trash. So the things that we throw away every day have more of an impact on the earth than the waste made by all of our businesses and industries. Every year, the hardworking people in waste management must remove more

The job of collecting waste is a big one. Workers collect huge amounts of trash every day.

than six hundred thousand whales worth of trash from our houses. Imagine going even a few weeks without waste management. Our streets and sidewalks would be piled high with garbage.

If trash collection stopped, the garbage would quickly become smelly, ugly, and inconvenient. It would also attract all sorts of pests and cause lots of serious health problems. Many years ago, plagues used to wipe out entire towns and cities. These illnesses were often brought on because of how people got rid of their waste.

The waste management system does not just dispose of household garbage. It is also responsible for properly disposing of hazardous and radioactive materials and polluted water. This helps us avoid all sorts of environmental disasters.

As you can see, good waste management systems are very important for every community. These systems can be very complex. They involve lots of different jobs, structures, and machines. In this book, we'll learn all about the history of waste management systems and how they've improved over the years. We'll look at the workers who build and operate the systems. We'll also find out about some of the most challenging waste management situations in America. Finally, we'll explore some of the brilliant ideas that scientists and engineers have come up with to make waste management even better in the future.

The next time you see your garbage collectors, make sure to thank them for keeping a whale-sized pile of trash out of your neighborhood! Now, let's roll back the clock and look at how waste management began.

Chapter 1

EARLY WASTE MANAGEMENT SYSTEMS

Most of the infrastructure systems we use today—like ports, dams, and bridges—were first invented thousands of years ago. But waste management is a fairly new idea. Let's look into the history of waste management and find out why!

Ancient Waste Management

Humans have always produced waste. But in the past, we produced much less of it. A few thousand years ago, communities were much smaller. There wasn't enough waste to cause problems for the villages and towns. People would store their waste, which was mostly ashes and food scraps, a short walk from their homes.

Then nature would take care of the rest.

Even in the very first cities, which had more people, waste management wasn't a big worry. Like waste that was made in smaller villages, almost all of the waste from ancient cities was biodegradable. This means it could be easily broken down by living

Before garbage trucks, there were horse-drawn wagons. Here, a trash pick-up wagon makes its rounds in Philadelphia.

things. Biodegradable waste is much easier to deal with than the man-made materials we throw away today. The cities had special areas for getting rid of waste. It would break down into soil quickly, so they rarely had to worry about it piling up.

Some ancient communities followed rituals to remove waste. One of the most interesting examples of this is the ancient Mayans. They were a group of people that lived in Central America. Every month, Mayan villagers would gather all of their waste and bring it to large dumps. There, the waste was burned. Today we use a similar method with a lot of our waste. We'll discuss that a little later.

When waste is disposed of incorrectly, it can lead to pollution. Air, water, or soil can be contaminated by substances in the waste that are harmful to living things. Today's waste management systems are designed to create as little pollution as possible. But in ancient times, people didn't understand the impact that their trash could have on the environment. A good example of this is the Nor Loch. This was a marsh located just outside of Edinburgh, Scotland, in the Middle Ages. At the time, Edinburgh was very crowded. People began to throw their garbage and sewage down a hill that led to the Nor Loch. The water became so polluted that it was unusable for any other purpose. The Nor Loch was eventually filled in to make way for new construction. If the people of ancient Edinburgh had been a little more careful with their waste, maybe they would have had another source of drinking water!

Waste Management During the Industrial Revolution

Waste management as we know it today really began during the Industrial Revolution. This was a period of major advances in the late 1700s and early 1800s. Lots of new buildings, factories, and machines were built. Cities started to become much more populated than ever before. The new factories created lots of waste and products that could not be broken down. There weren't any

All of the factories and businesses that opened during the Industrial Revolution made waste that needed to be disposed of.

Workers collect waste from factories in England.
They were known as dustmen.

systems in place to deal with all of the waste. The cities quickly became filthy and unhealthy.

Many of the biggest cities in the world at the time were in England. So it is no surprise that this is where waste management began. The earliest call for a system to be developed was in 1751. A London official named Corbyn Morris suggested that the city create a team whose job would be picking up the trash and dumping it outside of the city. This was a smart idea, but it didn't really catch on at the time.

Dust-yards were the original solid waste management system. They began appearing in London in the late 1700s. At the time, most of the city's waste was coal ash from the factories. They called this waste "dust." Dust was valuable because it could be used for making bricks and fertilizing crops. So all of the waste from nearby factories and homes would be dumped in a dust-yard. There, workers would separate the dust from everything else. They would then sell the dust to farmers and builders. They might keep, sell, or discard the other items they came across in the trash. Since it made a lot of money, the dust-yard system spread across the entire city. It worked fairly well as a form of waste management. In the mid-1850s, the value of dust collapsed and the dust-yards faded away. But the people of London hadn't seen the last of waste management systems.

Lucky Edwin Chadwick

Edwin Chadwick's idea to get rid of cholera by getting rid of the trash in the streets was brilliant. But did you know that he came up with it for the wrong reason? Chadwick believed that breathing in air that was polluted by rotting garbage caused disease. He wanted to remove the trash so that these invisible "clouds of disease" would go away. Today, we know that these clouds don't exist. We know that diseases are caused by germs that can live in rotting waste. It's a good thing that Chadwick's incorrect theory was so close to the correct one! Otherwise, it may have taken much longer for waste management to be started in England and around the world!

Over the next few decades, a horrible disease called cholera hit the city. This created a public health crisis. One of the people who tried to find a solution to the problem was a man named Edwin Chadwick. In 1842, he wrote a book called *The Sanitary Condition of the Labouring Population.* He argued that the health of the citizens would be much better if waste was removed and managed responsibly by the city. His plan was very popular. It led to the Nuisances Removal and Disease Prevention Act of 1846. This bill created the first modern waste management system!

The city of London knew that it needed to make some changes in waste management. A group of city workers was put in charge of the removal of waste. After a few years of trial and error, the Public Health Act of 1879 was passed. The new law greatly improved the waste management systems throughout England. This law required every home to get rid of their trash in movable containers. They were the world's first trash cans!

In the next chapter, we'll take a look at how far waste management systems have come since the nineteenth century.

Chapter 2

IMPROVING WASTE MANAGEMENT

People were starting to see that managing their waste would make their communities cleaner and healthier. Soon waste management systems began popping up all around the world. In 1895, New York became the first American city with a public waste management program.

As time went on, the number of people in cities and towns kept increasing. People made lots of new inventions. This meant lots of new materials. Many of these materials were hard to get rid of safely. Waste management became a bigger challenge. But technology has played a big role in improving waste management. Engineers and scientists have come up with better ways to collect,

Today, a lot of trash is burned at facilities like
the waste incinerator plant shown here.

transport, and remove waste. Let's take a look at some of the key parts of today's waste management systems.

How We Deal with Waste

We know that most of the waste created in cities and towns before the Industrial Revolution was biodegradable. This means that the main job of early waste management systems was to simply remove garbage from the streets. Once it was removed, half the battle was over. The waste would be dumped at a landfill. This is a place where people dispose of waste materials. Once the waste was at the landfill, it would be thrown in a pit or piled up. Then it would break down on its own. Today's landfills are a bit different. We bury the waste underground to help the waste break down faster. This also keeps everything as compact as possible.

After the Industrial Revolution, many things were made with metal and plastic. These materials can take years to break down and become soil. They started to clog up the landfills. It became clear that something would need to be invented to help get rid of the new kinds of waste. One of the first inventions that helped to solve the problem was the incinerator. An incinerator is a device that burns waste materials at very high temperatures. The materials are turned to ash. This ash is more biodegradable than the original materials. It is also much more compact. It can be added to landfills without taking up too much space.

The first incinerators were created in England by Albert Fryer. In 1874, he came up with his invention, which he called the "destructor." The incinerator was very simple. It had a huge furnace that would burn trash quickly. It also had a tall pipe called a flue. This released the exhaust (used gas) into the air. Incinerating waste reduces the original waste by up to 85 percent. This makes disposal much more convenient. But there was a problem. People knew almost nothing about pollution at the time. This meant that they didn't do anything to clean the flue gas that was made by the burning waste. Incinerators were spitting out poisonous smoke into the sky. It covered nearby areas with ash and made some of the people who breathed it in very sick.

A Short History of Garbage Trucks

The most basic part of waste management is collecting waste from homes and businesses. The earliest garbage trucks were open carts that were pulled by horses. As you can imagine, they were very smelly! They also worked slowly. In the early 1900s, garbage trucks became motorized. They also got roofs and a lever that would seal in the odors. Not long after that came the scooper. It could be filled with trash at ground level. Then it lifted the waste into the vehicle mechanically. In 1938, the Garwood Load Packer became the first garbage truck to use a hydraulic compactor to crush waste as it was being collected. This design is still in use around the world today!

For these reasons, the first incinerators were not very popular with the public.

Today, incineration is still one of the most common ways to manage waste. It is quite popular in places where there is not a lot of space, like Japan. Today's incinerators are much bigger than the earliest ones. Also, our technology has made them more efficient and safer for the environment. Modern incinerators burn a lot more waste at a much higher temperature. This means that they can handle tons and tons of waste every hour. The flue gas is cleaned by passing through a series of filters and scrubbers. These are designed to get rid of most of the harmful chemicals that are made by incineration.

Challenges of Hazardous Waste

In the past, all waste was treated the same way. It was either burned in incinerators or buried in landfills. But today, we have some materials that cannot be disposed of in this way. These things are either too dangerous or they cause too much pollution. Hazardous waste is any waste that could be a threat to public health or the environment. Waste management systems have created special ways to deal with such waste safely and responsibly.

Hazardous waste doesn't just come from huge factories. Smaller businesses like dry cleaners and automobile repair shops also create different kinds of hazardous waste. This waste cannot be put

Most garbage trucks today have some kind of compactor that moves and crushes the trash to make room for the next load.

Workers who clean up hazardous waste must use equipment and clothing to protect themselves.

into the garbage can with the rest of the trash. Instead, it is stored in special containers. Then it is picked up by waste management workers who are trained in hazardous waste removal. Then, the hazardous waste is taken to a disposal facility. There, it is treated to make it safer to dispose of.

Some hazardous waste is not as dangerous as others. The less dangerous types can often be treated and made into a solid. Then they can be placed in landfills without fear of contaminating the surrounding area. Some hazardous waste can even be burned in special furnaces that make sure no toxic gases escape into the air. Then, the ashes can be placed in landfills with the rest of the waste.

One of the most interesting kinds of hazardous waste is nuclear waste. This is waste that contains radioactive material. It often comes from nuclear power plants or scientific research. This material is extremely dangerous for humans and the environment. It must be disposed of very carefully. Nuclear waste is often placed in concrete and stored underground, far away from people. The most toxic nuclear waste can't even be stored near the earth's surface. It is buried at least 1,000 (305 meters) feet below the ground!

You've learned about the many advances in waste management. Now let's take a closer look at how waste management systems work to help the environment.

Chapter 3

SUSTAINABILITY

You've learned a lot about the different ways that we dispose of waste. But this is only one part of today's waste management. In fact, incinerating waste and burying it in landfills is usually the last resort for getting rid of waste. This is because one of the main goals of waste management is sustainability. That means that we try to avoid using up our natural resources. Sustainability is very important for the environment. In this chapter, we'll take a closer look at how we keep waste management as sustainable as possible.

The Three Rs

The most important idea behind sustainable waste management is called the waste hierarchy. A hierarchy is a group of things that are ranked. So in the waste hierarchy, the different ways of dealing with waste are ranked from most desirable to the least desirable. You have probably already heard of the first three points in this hierarchy: reduce, reuse, recycle.

Recyclable materials often go to a recycling center like this one. Here, the materials are sorted into different types before being recycled.

The best thing that we can do for the environment is to make less waste in the first place. In other words, we should *reduce* the amount of stuff we throw away. Companies can help a lot with this step. They can use as little packaging as possible for their products. They can make things that last a long time. They can also use biodegradable or recyclable materials that don't create as much pollution. Consumers (like you) can help by buying only things that they need. They can try to buy things that are packaged in a sustainable way. They can also buy second-hand items when possible. Instead of going to the mall, they can shop for clothes at thrift stores and buy used electronics online.

After reducing comes *reusing.* Instead of buying something new, it is better to reuse the one you have if it still works. If it doesn't work, try to repair it. Another type of reuse is using something for a different purpose than what you first bought it for. For example, many people throw away or recycle plastic soda bottles. But there are so many cool things you can do with them! Just one idea is to make a flower holder. With an adult's help, cut out part of the side of the bottle. Fill it up with soil and plant your flowers! Reusing waste means that you are helping the earth. You also get to complete fun do-it-yourself projects at the same time.

By reducing and reusing, waste never makes it to waste management in the first place. This is the best possible case for the environment. The third method in the waste hierarchy is *recycling.*

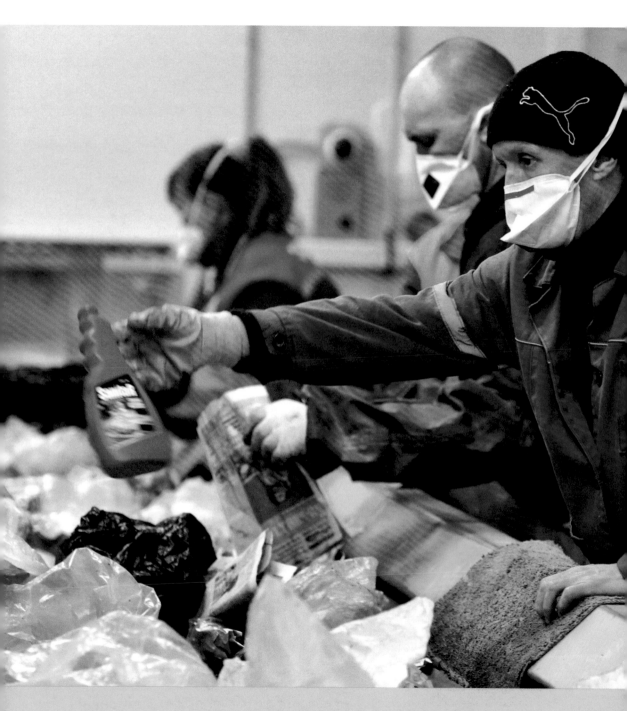

Workers at a recycling center sort through plastic materials.

Single-Stream Recycling

To make recycling easier, some areas have started a single-stream recycling system. In this system, you put everything that can be recycled into one big container. Then workers sort through it all at a recycling facility. This ensures that nothing is wasted and recycling is as convenient as possible. Studies have shown that when a city or town starts single-stream recycling, more people recycle.

This means changing waste materials into new materials. Recycling isn't quite as good as eliminating waste entirely. But when you recycle, you make sure that your waste can help make new materials, instead of ending up in a landfill.

Recycling is a pretty complicated process. Different materials need to be separated from one another before they can be changed into a new material. The way that this is done changes from place to place. In most places, people have to sort their recycling on their own. They tie up their newspapers and cardboard. They separate plastics from metals and glass. Then they leave them on the curb for recycling or bring them to a sorting facility.

Waste-to-Energy

Sometimes waste cannot be reduced, reused, or recycled. In those cases, waste heads to the incinerator or the landfill. But engineers and scientists have come up with ways to use these systems to create new energy. This helps to reduce the environmental impact in other areas, like power plants. This idea is called waste-to-energy.

As you learned earlier, incinerating waste makes ash, gases, and heat. The ashes are placed in landfills. But in the past, nothing was done with the gases and the heat. Today, we have learned how to capture the heat and gases and turn them into electricity. One of the ways that this is done is by using the heat from burning waste to boil water. This powers steam generators that produce electricity. This electricity is then directed through power plants and used to power nearby homes and businesses. Since it is an extra source of power, fewer fuels like gas need to be burned to keep a town or city running. Of course, this is good for the environment.

There is even more that we can do to use the gases that are made by burning waste. These gases can be changed into usable fuels, like methane and ethanol. This is a fairly new idea, but it could have a major impact on sustainability once more people start to use it. We'll learn more about this and other new waste management techniques in chapter 5.

You're up-to-date on the latest improvements in waste management. Now let's focus on the most important part of any infrastructure system: the workers!

Chapter 4

WHO WORKS IN WASTE MANAGEMENT?

Years ago, waste management was pretty simple. Workers would go around town and collect waste from homes and businesses. Then they would bring the waste to a nearby landfill. There, they would either throw it into a pile, burn it, or bury it. These jobs didn't require much special training. But they were hard work. Moving all of that heavy trash took a lot of strong workers!

As time went on, technology improved. New machines made getting rid of waste much easier. But the amount of waste keeps growing year after year. Non-biodegradable materials need to be dealt with very carefully. On top of that, we now understand much more about pollution and sustainability. These add new concerns to

A worker sifts through garbage at a landfill.

Trucks with mechanical arms make trash and
recycling collection much easier.

waste management that just didn't exist before! Let's take a look at some of the old and new careers in waste management.

Trash Collection: The Original Waste Management Career

The most basic job in waste management has always been collecting waste from homes and businesses and moving it to a waste management facility. In the past, trash was piled onto horse-drawn carriages. Large teams of workers were needed to do this. Some would direct the carriage, while others would gather the trash from the street. When they arrived at the landfill, they would all help to dump the materials there. Then they traveled back into town to collect more waste. Aside from a few people who ran the landfills, this was basically the only career in waste management.

Today, things are much easier for workers. Improvements to garbage trucks mean that much more waste can be collected in a single trip. Even better, garbage trucks can now be operated by only two or three people. All they need is the driver and one or two workers to collect waste and throw it into the back of the truck. This means that just a few people are able to do more work than nearly a dozen workers could manage a century ago.

But technology has gone even further in improving how waste is collected. Some garbage trucks now have crane arms that the

Working at a Landfill

One physical career in waste management is working at a landfill. As you just learned, landfill jobs used to be done by trash collectors. But as time went on, landfills became larger and more complex. A team of workers would work at a landfill full-time. They hauled and buried waste by hand or using basic tools. This is another area of waste management that has been improved by technology. Today, one bulldozer operator can move and bury much more waste in a single day than an entire team of laborers could handle in a week!

driver can operate with a joystick. This allows them to pick up garbage cans and empty them into their trucks without ever leaving the driver's seat. This means that work that used to be done by two or three people a decade ago can now be done by a single person!

In the near future, even more things will become automated. This means that cars and trucks will be able to drive themselves. Some test vehicles are already on the road today. When this happens, garbage trucks will be able to pick up trash and deliver it to waste management facilities without anyone on board! This will mean that soon there will be no need for garbage men and women. But don't worry! There are plenty of other waste management careers that are becoming more and more important as time goes on.

Workers at landfills often operate heavy machinery like this loader.

Environmental Careers in Waste Management

Most of today's careers in waste management did not even exist until recently. These are the careers that involve sustainability and environmental science. More and more, waste management has to do with protecting our environment. Waste management is the fastest-growing career path in all of environmental studies.

Environmental engineers work to protect the environment by cutting down on waste and pollution. These engineers can have lots of different specialty areas. They work at every level of waste management. These workers oversee waste management facilities and check that they are running well. They also make sure that the facilities are up to environmental standards. There is a different kind of engineer for every single area of waste management. These include resource recovery (recycling waste instead of burying it), environmental compliance (following the rules), and sustainability.

There are also many scientists and engineers whose job is to come up with new ways to dispose of waste that are better for the Earth. They study every part of waste management facilities. Then they find ways that emissions can be reduced. They also try to find new ways to reuse waste and save resources. Like environmental engineers, these workers specialize in very certain areas of waste management. They might be experts on waste water or aluminum recycling. Then all of the scientists and engineers from other areas can come together to create the waste management systems of tomorrow!

By now, you've learned a whole lot about the waste management systems of the past. You've also seen how technology has improved the systems today. In our final chapter, we'll take a look at some of the most interesting and impressive ideas for the future of waste management. Some of them are already happening in certain places around the world. Others are just ideas that won't become reality until technology improves. But all of them could have a huge impact on the way that future generations handle their waste!

Chapter 5

THE WASTE MANAGEMENT SYSTEMS OF TOMORROW

Throughout this book, you have seen how waste management has changed from simple teams of trash collectors to the cutting edge of environmental science. And this has all happened in less than 150 years! You've learned how technology has made these systems more sustainable. You've also seen the effects that automation will have on some of the careers in waste management.

All of these areas will keep improving as time goes on. Facilities will become more and more efficient. More areas of the field will become automated. Emissions will be reduced further and further.

Today, it is easier than ever for people to
dispose of trash responsibly.

These improvements are all extremely important to the future of
waste management. But we are going to cover something a bit
different in this chapter. If you use your imagination, you can easily
figure out how these changes will affect waste management.

Instead, this chapter is going to focus on the longshots. We will
look at the ideas that seemed crazy only a few decades ago—
and a few that might seem crazy today. These are the extreme
ideas that could totally change the way we think about waste. So
let's explore some of the most exciting concepts in the world of
waste management!

Trash Power!

You learned a little bit about waste-to-energy in chapter 3. The heat that is made by incinerators is sometimes changed into electricity. This helps to make incinerating more sustainable—in this case, it saves power. Some bright minds in waste management have taken this basic idea and run with it. Their idea? Turning trash into fuel.

Imagine if we could create trash-powered machines. This would have a huge, positive impact on the environment. In the waste hierarchy, we would be moving waste-to-energy incineration from step four all the way up to step two: reusing! Also, if your car runs on waste that was made from trash, that means it *doesn't* run on fossil fuels. Burning fossil fuels is not good for the environment. Even better, fossil fuels—and most of the resources we might use to replace them—are very limited. But we have a literally endless supply of trash!

These benefits of turning trash into fuel are so great that some of the smartest scientists and engineers in the world are working on the idea. One way is called gasification. In this method, waste is placed in extremely high temperatures with a careful balance of air and steam. This is done until the waste is changed into a mixture of common elements called syngas. Syngas can be used in fuel cells or gas engines. It can also be mixed with other materials to create different fuels. Gasification is a very new idea. It's only

At this modern waste plant, waste is heated up
to be used for different kinds of fuel.

Pyrolysis

Pyrolysis is a lot like gasification. But instead of making fuel to be used in normal engines, pyrolysis heats up organic materials in a vacuum in order to create energy. This means it could be used to turn materials such as animal waste and sawdust into fuel. Pyrolysis could also be quite useful for recycling tires. Landfills are full of tires, which are not biodegradable and take up a lot of space. Tire pyrolysis would create more fuel and more space in landfills. Pyrolysis can also change plastics back into oil! While it isn't as popular as gasification, pyrolysis could certainly change the way that certain types of waste are processed.

being put into practice in a few places. But if scientists can find a way to do it at a low enough cost, it could totally change several industries at once.

A World with Zero Waste

The goal of every waste management system has been to reduce the amount of waste that is needlessly thrown away every year. A lot has been done to reach that goal. People have been taught about the risks of using and discarding too much "stuff." Recycling programs have become common in most areas. And more people are interested in living a sustainable life. Together, these things have already done a lot to reduce the amount of waste we create.

Lots of progress has been made with waste management. It's up to everyone to pitch in to keep the earth safe, healthy, and free of trash.

Americans still produce more waste per person than any other country in the world. But recently this trend has been changing. In 2000, about 4.75 pounds pounds (2.1 kg) of waste was created by each person. Today's levels are nearly a half-pound lower per person. Hopefully these good habits will continue and we will make less and less waste.

Many environmental scientists and activists believe that our goal should be a world with zero waste. This would mean that every material is reused and nothing is sent to incinerators or landfills. This is a great goal, but is it possible? Maybe not around the world. There are too many materials we haven't found a way to reuse yet. But as technology continues to change and improve, we will figure out ways to reuse more. Even more importantly, as time goes on, hopefully people will start to understand why living a sustainable life is so important.

Even though zero waste throughout the world isn't realistic today, individual people can certainly live zero-waste lives. It isn't easy to do. It means giving up many of the conveniences of the modern world. But if people are determined to cut their environmental impact, it can be done. These people are truly doing their part to change the planet. They are good role models for anyone who is interested in improving their own relationship with the environment.

CHRONOLOGY

Circa 250 Ancient Mayans begin to burn their waste in large dumps.

1751 Corbyn Morris suggests that London create a waste management team.

Circa 1790 The first dust-yards appear in London, England.

1842 Edwin Chadwick publishes *The Sanitary Condition of the Labouring Population*.

1846 The Nuisance Removal and Disease Prevention Act of 1846 creates the first modern waste management system.

1874 Albert Fryer patents his design for the world's first incinerator.

1879 The Public Health Act of 1879 improves waste management throughout England and creates the first residential garbage can system.

1895 The first American waste management program begins in New York City.

1938 The Garwood Load Packer is invented.

2000 The United States produces the most waste in human history: 4.74 pounds of waste per person per day.

2002 Electronic waste grows faster than any other type of waste in the European Union.

2016 After several years of investing in the technology, China controls a total of 434 waste-to-energy plants.

2020 The city of San Francisco pledges to be zero waste by this year.

GLOSSARY

biodegradable Able to be easily broken down by microorganisms.

dust-yard Areas where solid waste was dumped and sorted so coal ash could be gathered for use in brickmaking and farming; one of the earliest waste management systems.

emissions Gases or other chemicals that are given off when something is burned.

flue A tall pipe for releasing the exhaust from a furnace into the atmosphere.

hazardous waste Any waste that is a potential threat to public health or the environment.

incinerator A device for burning waste materials at very high temperatures until they are reduced to ash.

Industrial Revolution A period of major advances in industry in the late 1700s and early 1800s.

landfill A site for the disposal of waste materials, either by burying them or leaving them in a pit or pile.

municipal solid waste Household garbage and trash.

nuclear waste Waste that contains radioactive material.

pollution The contamination of air, water, or soil by substances that are harmful to living organisms.

recycling The process of converting waste materials into new materials and objects.

sustainability Avoiding the depletion of natural resources in order to help the environment.

waste Unwanted or unusable materials that need to be discarded.

waste management The collection, transportation, treatment, and disposal of waste.

FURTHER READING

Books

Labrecque, Ellen. *Recycling and Waste*. Ann Arbor, MI: Cherry Lake, 2017.

Mulder, Michelle. *Trash Talk: Moving Toward a Zero-Waste World*. Custer, WA: Orca Books, 2015.

Newman, Patricia. *Plastic, Ahoy! Investigating the Great Pacific Garbage Patch*. Minneapolis, MN: Millbrook Press, 2016.

Rhatigan, Joe. *Get a Job at the Landfill*. Ann Arbor, MI: Cherry Lake, 2016.

Websites

eSchool Today: Waste Management

www.eschooltoday.com/waste-recycling/waste-management-tips-for-kids.html

Find out about all of the different kinds of waste and recycling.

Kids Ecology: Waste Disposal

www.kidsecologycorps.org/our-environment/natural-cycles/waste-disposal

Learn more about waste and find out how you can help the environment.

INDEX